ETHEREAL ESCAPES

ETHEREAL ESCAPES

ANTHOLOGY

Alisha Rehman
Hania Faheem

Printed: September, 2023
Edition: 1st
ISBN: 978-969-749-257-2
Price: Rs 1400 PKR, $10 US

www.auraqpublications.com | raabta@auraqpublications.com
@AuraqPublications | @AuraqBooks | +92-300-0571-530
Printed and Bound by ***Passive Printers*** - www.passiveprinters.com

For those who hold their scars dear,
you are stronger than the will of the sun.

Contents

- **When You Bleed Black**

by Alisha rehman

- **Ink of the soul**

by Abdul Basit

- **Hushed Heartaches**

by Faqiha Farheen

- **When Life Gives You Lemons...**

by Fakeha Imran

- **Veiled Reveries**

by Hania

- **The Suffocating Muse**

by Misbah Gul

- **Arcana of the Heart**

by Qania Murtaza

- **Unwoven Tapestries**

by Sarah Malik

- **Symphonies of a Somber Soul**

by Ukasha Wadood

When You Bleed Black
By Alisha Rehman

Dance of ice and fire

The flowing darkness within those curls,
Those curious, daring twilight eyes.
Purple hyacinth crowning her pride.
I believe it was a siren in the hide.

Look there as she moves delicately,
Around the battlefield of desire.
An executioner punishing with every swirl.
Making me want to tell,
About the heart which was on fire.

But I believe the need not remain, but desire,
My doll in the strings of Moira.
Won't it be delightful to be stabbed?
In heart by those frail hands.
But I am the sun who will never fade.

The cruel, the devil, the puppeteer,
My nemesis was born in nowhere.
His only desire is to cage the dove,
Pity that it's not a bird but a beast,
Sharpening its claws in sleep.

Dance of ice and fire

The one you want to tame,
The one who sends you wolfsbane.
Is a bird of life that desires to survive,
Under the clouds of someone else's pride.

Though birds welcoming like water is,
But remember the ice it never forgives.

So let's begin this ballet,
On the floor of roses and thorns.
Ice and fire may not bow,
But amalgam may cause something odd.

Nor future was icy like the moon.
Nor past was fiery like the sun.
The fates will collide,
Just as we, in tandem, move.

Though one shall fall, and one shall rise.

The dragon and the knights

Three knights stood tall and brave
Watching their death wake with grace
"You little fools, are you not afraid?"
The dragon asked, full of hate
"No, we are not," a unison scream,
"The goddess Tyche had blessed us with new feats".
"Let me hear what it blessed you with,
Or was it a new delusion put in?"
O, I, you lame creature, was gifted knowledge
I know every being which walks on four.
then the second man rose with pride
O, I, your stupid creature, was gifted power,
Embedded into my sword is a gift from heaven.
Oh, I see what amazing beings,
So, what were you gifted, the last knight?
The man shuddered at the words but did not move
because he knows what is true.
O, I, the magnificent dragon, was gifted future.
My powers crossed the realms of existence,
Looking for all possibilities of what was due.
"So, you know what I know," the dragon whispered
breaking the distance like a snake,
playing with the fear of the third's fate.

The dragon and the knights

the dragon's tail enveloped the third knight.
"I know what you know," the knight whispered.
The dragon smiled, eyes turned to a deathly glare.
casting a breath so icy, a death no one can escape
The mountains shivered with dragon's might.
fate was sealed, frozen to their feet
two men laid like fallen sticks
The third one looked at the upcoming fate
"So Tyche, give you the curse
The curse of fear
O how I love to see you die in pain
But I am not filled with emotion so disdain
So go away till you see the sun
Because fear always eats the men's fate".

Wait

There is this space,
Waiting to be filled.
I wait for you in a daze.
For countless days and nights.
To see just a glimpse,
Whether you are still alive.
The cold never forgives.
The heat always seeps,
In the bones who wait,
Starting from the windowsill.
I think I have gone old,
decades had passed,
Since I got the last glimpse.
Don't you like these dandelions?
Which my field grows.
Or the sunset I dream daily for,
It has been so long,
Since I got the last glimpse.
My house is now broken like a doll,
The field has grown wild.
All my known are dead.
Just like me as I sit,
On the broken windowsill.

Fear

The dead king's throne
All hail from the foe
The blood, the gore
All the jewelry disowned
The curse which grows
To the fence of mountains below,
unhedged remain the territory of Ghouls
How one can stay pure, not fowl
"I am the king," the titan declare
no foe remains and no king sustain
the power I have, the magic I possessed,
All who survived bow down to your knees
Might you have forgotten the decrease
But carve it in your sacred stones
The fear so delicious to not crave

A smile to die for

Can you smile every day,
Because it brightens my day.
I die to hear you laugh.
And The way your eyes glitter.
It just burns my heart with heat,
The eternal flame of bliss.
The honey-coated eyes.
Capturing the sun in its wake,
Is one to sell one's soul for.
Then won't it be a catastrophe?
When a tear escapes,
The hold of the blinding sun.
How can one reverse the pearl,
When it had left the attorney.
How can I hear the laugh?
When the skies turn grey.
Let the raindrops,
Let the sorrow fill the world.
Let the pain seep deep,
Cuz I don't care about pain.
Just the memory of the smile remains.
O how I desire your smile,
O dear one, let me tear the sky.
For you, I will make it possible,
For you, let me change the tides.
The tears from you.
Precious than all diamonds and pearls,
Just don't let them fall.
Just laugh the way you do,
I will be there at your back to support
Make those mistakes of yours
A solid base for you to stand
Because you are not fighting alone
you are now not one but more

To learn from fall

Sometimes one should break
To know how his muscle connects
Sometimes one should die
To learn the meaning of life
Sometimes one should lose everything
To see what really mattered
In the mere life span, he had

A child of hope and misery

The light rustle of leaves
With the delicate touch of sunlight
Move across your skin
Enveloping you in a motherly warmth
You lose the space of time.
As the darkness rise
Across the skies of light,
You wish to live more
When the nightshade bloom
In the cold of night.

Thief

There was one wish
just one wish to live
A desire to breathe,
But the wishes don't become real
As well as dreams
So that's how I died
When breathing had to be stolen.

Hunger of predator

A beast upon the prey
That predatory look conveyed
The heart clenched in a fist
That's how life turned into a mist
I feel that gaze now and then
Searching for something
O the gaze which holds the sun,
Burns every inch which is captured
O That darkness it conceals
the sharpness presenting the decree
Fall on your knees
Bend your bows
Or I shall choose
The fate of your
These words just dwell
Through the gaze
The prey failed
But the predator remained

Man made

Do we lie to you?
To whom we belong
From whom the stars envy
And sky mischief with
How can we lie to the one?
Who holds our hearts and fate?
As if we didn't die
When we saw the glimpse
Of that deadly face
A beauty that kills
With one gaze, it seems
One may find it useless
To create the weapons
World made like a seamstress
In the end, man-made is labeled
And God made us thrive.

Anonymous guide

There is a little balloon
Flying everywhere with me, following
flowing with wonders and secrets.
The one who got the power
To change the fates
O red little balloon, I saw you that day
You were talking with the sun
But you were not pleased
O red balloon, what you told the moon?
He was so happy
That he made the night so silvery
Like anyone could have ever seen
O red little balloon why the clouds cried when they saw you
Is there something I need to know?
O red little balloon, did you forget?
That I was waiting ahead for u

Broken doll

I wish I could mend you
Piece by piece and bone by bone
No flaw will be, no stitch missed
You will see how I merrily
Change you from bone to flesh
No need for makeup
No need for care
Cuz you, a dress-up doll
I will play with it every day

Bone's Desire

My heart's desired need
Need to be free
Need to be alive
Something I never feel
Though the dark clouds
Submerging the never-ending sky
I believe in the last ray
Which will Peirce through the sky
Reaching through the mountains and valleys
Across my bleeding heart
Tearing the soft flesh
Filling the void with light
I will feel complete, so divine.

A monster?

A sick boy looking through a glass window from the hospital bed. The sight to be seen was limited but enough for making him not go insane from the white walls but this time actually there was something to see, a lion was walking inside the fences of the medical sanctuary. In the other instance, he saw his parents come Inside the room. Wasn't it strange that the lion attacked at the same time his father's hand was raised at his mother?

A light in dark

In the darkest night,
The thunder reigns.
The heat of a newborn,
In a never-ending pain.
In such fear and terror,
One light originates,
Embracing the child warmly,
Solace what the offspring find.
A taste sweeter than honey
Warmer than the sun's light.

A poisonous tongue

Pledged destined oath crushed,
futile this virulent tongue,
splintered fame prevails

Bleeding sins

Pink cherry blossom,
Stood I jilted, rueing sins,
bleeding for mercy.

Devil footsteps

Walking in the footsteps of the devil,
I tread a path of darkness and sin.
The air is thick with the stench of evil,
And the ground beneath me quivers within.

The flames of hell flicker all around,
As I move through this treacherous terrain.
The cries of lost souls make a deafening sound,
Their agony, a never-ending pain.

The devil's whispers fill my mind,
A tempting voice beckons me near.
But I know the dangers that I'll find,
If I succumb to his deceitful sneer.

I walk with caution, step by step,
In this world of shadows and despair.
For I know that I must not forget,
My faith and my morals, my shield and my prayer.

And so I journey on this wicked road,
With the devil as my guide and foe.
But with the light of faith as my abode,
I know that I'll find my way out, whole.

Patience

Believe in yourself that you can be anything, anything which can mend your heart but remember whine is always majestic when stored longer.

Tainted crimson past

I feel it; I see it.
The rhythm of the grudge
The power to take the power to smudge
Blood has merged in the thirsty land
No fate has lasted till the peace had cast
No lives to take when no being alive
Just the broken glass of the past.

An evolving poison

I feel nothing
As my heart hurts,
Looks like my soul is draining
As my emotions have left
Creating a void for something else
Who could have thought
I got a taste of ruling
One could have taunted
But believe me
I will eat that man raw
I don't have the power
But it is just a matter of time
I will get it done
Whenever I completed my way,
Though it is a long journey
But I don't care
I do not bear kings
I make them
A born heir is as good as dead
We need a little poison
To make one resistant to poison itself.

A plea to stay

There was only one word
One word she wanted
to say in those ears
Wishing she could have
When he left her alone,
Standing in the damp
As the darkness enveloped her frame,
She felt nothing
Not even a sting of pain
Like the weeds grow
Stronger day by day
Like Belladonna, killing
Within second a fate
Nothing could grow too then!
Into something not born for free
She stood there
She did felt nothing
But the time didn't stop
She came to bloom
How could she know?
She wasn't a sunflower
The day was not hers; it was night
She was a moonflower
Born for light, was not her right

A born demon

Silent whispers were making me go insane. One word, just one word they were demanding, they desired; they were hungry. But for what you ask? It was food, but what food can satisfy this hunger? It doesn't want something easy to take. Something you can find in a supermarket or a shop. It requires blood, not to eat but to see, to fill the image with the colors of red. The food comes after the image, the feast of fear. I am going insane in a void of eternal darkness. I can only think of one thing. If I really take rest in this eternal void, what the demon will do when no chains will hold it back? I know the answer. It will devour.

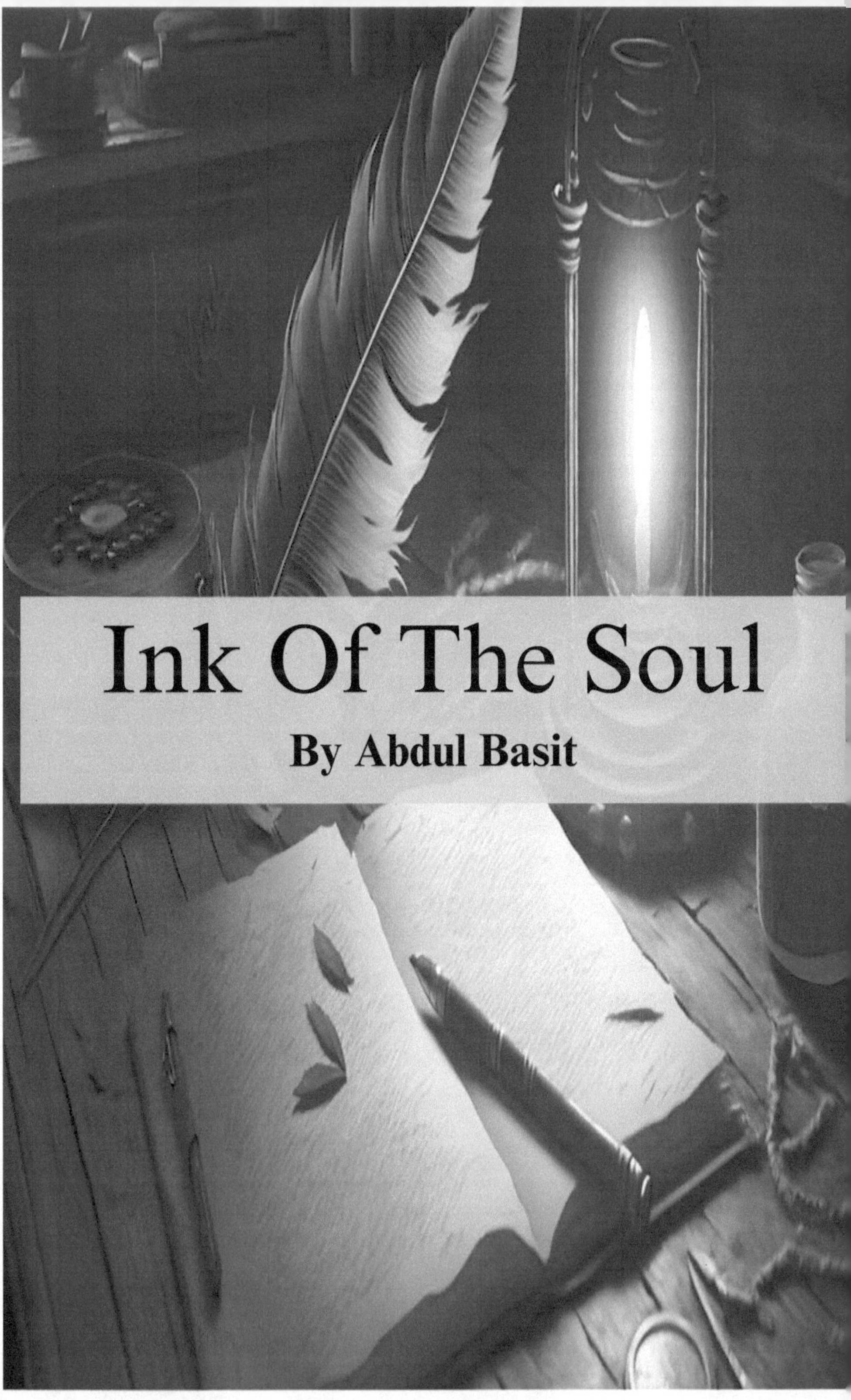

Ink Of The Soul

By Abdul Basit

Every day As Soon As

Every day, as soon as the beams drift,
the ripples of your memories make me rift.

Every day, as soon as I see your eyes,
the craving to live long heightens.

Every day, as soon as my heart fills with light,
the mind digs your remembrance in bright.

Every day, as soon as the ocean tides sour,
these lethargic eyes seek you on the shore.

Every day, with the birth of the new moon,
your fragile smile makes my heart long for hope.

Just like every day, the fragrance of flowers flutters,
life is blessed by the dawn of your character.

Love, a Play

Love, an everlasting play,
That ev'ry bod must display.
It's a texture that makes beats tickle,
And creates in every moment a chortle.
Fills the eyes with a sparkle,
And makes eager hearts twinkle.
In youth, it fetches a serene breeze,
And a smile puts restless souls at ease.
It revamps the rose with its presence,
And feeds its fragrance across a distance.
Love is like a delightful ray,
That ev'ry bod feels one day.

Apathetic Corpse Would Be Telling God

There were seven billion living dead bodies
All were friends, they were frauds

I was the only one suffering from insanity
By God, all the others were willing

Each breath was heavy on me
Who were they who were free?

Yes, civilization was a slang word
On whose name there were all contradictions

The exception for those who bowed
Pain for those who declined.

I Shall Speak, I Shall Write

Why should I stay silent?
How long shall I behold my ruin's bitter play?
And dwell on a fearful past in endless disarray?
I am not like a lost ink to stay hushed.

I too want to think about my future,
I too want to achieve my intents,
I too want to support the poor and needy,
I too want to become an aid for the helpless.

Why should I stay silent?
How long shall I leave my present to its sorry state?
How long should I keep remembering the days gone by?
I'm not like a flower to stay silent.

I too want to defend my land,
I too want to roam freely in it,
I too want to toil for its survival,
I too want to contribute to its progress.

Why should I stay silent?
Now I shall speak, I shall write,
Even though my song is bitter, there is loyalty within its
depth.

Igniting Revolt

Within each soul, rebellion's flame,
Dreaming for the uprising, we proclaim.

A desire deep, evolution's creed,
To sow the seeds of a world freed.

In togetherness, we walk out and swear,
Injustice and oppression, we'll repair.

With bravery as our beacon bright,
We'll stand resolute, challenging the twilight.

I Am Unlimited

I am the spring harvest of impunity,
There are no restraints, I am unlimited.
I am a cyclone of consciousness,
I am a desireless light, beginningless.

I am autumn in illusion, spring in sight,
I am an aimless journey, an unintended trip.
I am the endless bloom of green,
I am the unfolding voice of a dream.

I am the far-reaching light, limitless radiance,
I am the unfading beacon, hope for hearts,
I am a star, glimmering on heights,
I am the restless moon of nights.

I am always a new color, a new voice,
There are no limits, I am unlimited.

Unveiling the Mystique of Desert Me

In those scorching dunes,
Where camels' known as jet
There's no mobile or internet
There they live, in peaceful communes.

They need not camp during the day
As their camels surely know the way
Under a night full of stars bright
They navigate by celestial light.

Their hearts as vast as love's rise,
For them, the adventure never dies
In the desert hush profound
They gather around the fire's mound.

They reminisce in melancholy songs,
Sassi-Punnu-like, timeless love tales prolong.

Unveiling The Mystique of Desert Women

The eyes kept meeting with shepherdesses, on the way
As war food, their loved ones had gone across the bay.

Yet their solitaries were devoid of all notions of sin
The lamps of their modesty were shining on their chin.

In those flowers, strength failed to meet a stare so bold
Concealing faces, lids shielded eyes from tales untold.

They grazed goats in the burning desert, all-day
And used to remember their heartthrobs in a musical way.

The music was so wonderful that whoever heard it
Would recall Moses and the Shepherds, their story's
summit.

life's last chapter is like a bulky novel

In the darkness of night, my loneliness is a fighter
Battling my achievements, making my future brighter.
The last Medal I received was like the last gate of heaven
Ingress is certain, but for those who are wiser.

The last sip of wine, the last job of tribal marine
the last chapter of life, with full hope and desire.
When I don't have a shoulder to cry, woods with fire
I am Chimpanzee Not a Champ, YOU were a liar, you ARE a liar

I am not a fighter. I don't have a future brighter nor am I wiser
Like the false character of a novel, I am a coward; a liar.

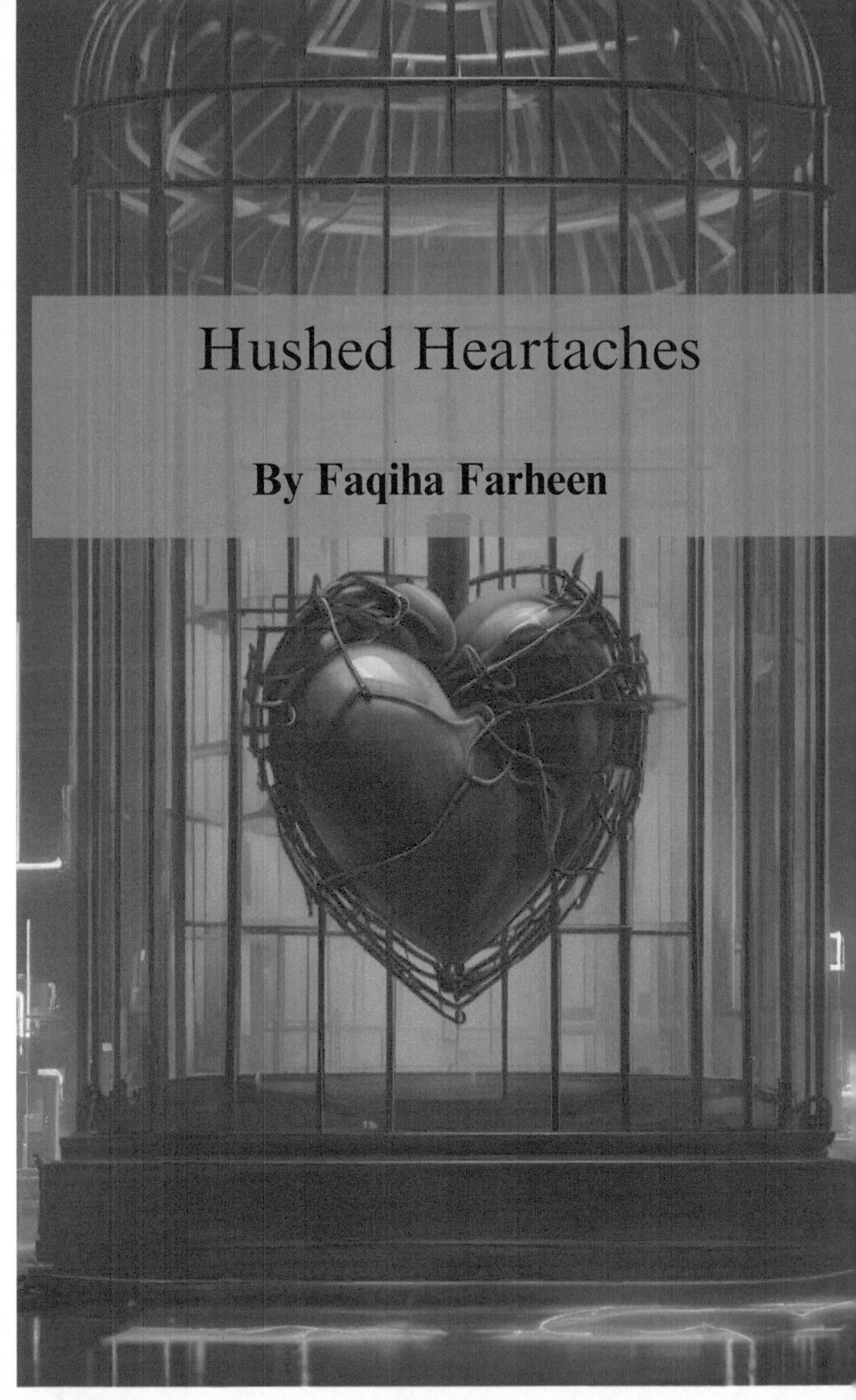
Hushed Heartaches
By Faqiha Farheen

The clock ticks at 1:46 am, a burden on my heart,
Suffocated, longing for breath to start.
Air insufficient, unable to cry,
The void in my chest, I can't deny.

The beast lives within me, memories entwined,
Each second spent near you, etched in my mind.
A 'thing' you made, can't love, can't hate,
But I smile, though not pure, it's my trait.

Unbreathing, staring at the roof, eyes dry,
Songs that make others weep, I wonder why.
Heart still beats, yearning for peace,
Tears gather, my emotions release.

Filled with salty water, tears run free,
Months without crying, I wonder at myself.
Tragedy, not the cause, but the change,
When did I become like this, so estranged?

Icy winds bite my veins,
Their frost invading emotion's waves.
As the chill seeps deeper into my core,
I welcome and embrace the cold
Like winter's touch upon my soul's terrain,
It numbs the ache and eases the emotional strain.
With each frozen gust that caresses my skin,
I find an icy release, a soothing within.
Nature's grasp, both harsh and tender,
In the icy release, I find a moment to surrender.

When I see the sun descending in the sky's sea,
My heart sinks, feeling weak and lonely.
Yearning for a loved one, to sit with me,
As we both sink, find solace and harmony.

With the moon's white glow, the sky adorned,
Focus fades, and emotions are adorned.
Three of you, Sun, Moon, and you,
My heart melts like a candle, feelings askew.

Your beauty, divine, hard to comprehend,
Which one melts me more, I can't apprehend.
Rhythmic dance of elements, nature's art,
In your presence, I find peace in my heart.

Horror, a tranquil ocean, beneath the moon's glow,
Lies silent and calm, its depths in shadow.
But when waves come, it stirs with chilling might,
The heart races fast, gripped by fear's bite.

Yet as waves subside, it hides once more,
Lurking beneath the surface, quiet in its core.
Patiently waiting, for the next wave's play,
To rise again, and send shivers our way.

Like a leading male, I move with you,
We dance in tune, beneath the moon.
One hand on your shoulder, the other holds your hand,
We glide on steps you command
I walk into the space you leave behind,
Singing the lyrics of the song you designed,
Yet hand in hand, with each step I take,
Feeling suffocated, my heart does ache.

You, the puppeteer, and I, the puppet on rings,
Dancing to your tune, like a bird that sings,
I weave emotions, my melodies profound,
The more I hurt, the more enchanting they sound.
As I sing, hurt turns into art,
And you, amused, hold a puppet's heart.

Regret eats a person from inside, unseen,
Till touched, they shatter, like glass, so keen.
Sharpy, edgy, fierce, hungry for a hunt,
Baring its fangs, waiting for a desert.
It can wound anyone who dares to touch,
No tenderness shown, mercy it won't clutch.
At the hands of these feeble yet solid crystals,
Regret's relentless grip, on your chest rests.

Face covered with tears, consumed by anger,
A tempest brewing, a storm that's no stranger.
This tempest's wrath, in a cup erupting,
Like a volcano's fury, it's darkly tempting.
Drink it down, rage unfulfilled,
Destroying within, with hate and resentment distilled.

Remembering every face that crossed my way,
The unreachable things I had, slipped away.
Good people I never cherished, now lost,
Escaped through my hand, at a heavy cost.
Scars on my body from thorns that pierced,
The bad people I met, their marks preserved
Time took its course, now I stand alone,
In the desert, no flower in sight, overgrown.

You're moving too fast, my friend,
I try to be by your side, till the end,
Running with short legs, I race to keep up,
I'm out of breath while I strive to catch up.
A favor, I seek, and I know it may be a lot,
Can you crawl with me, just for a thought?

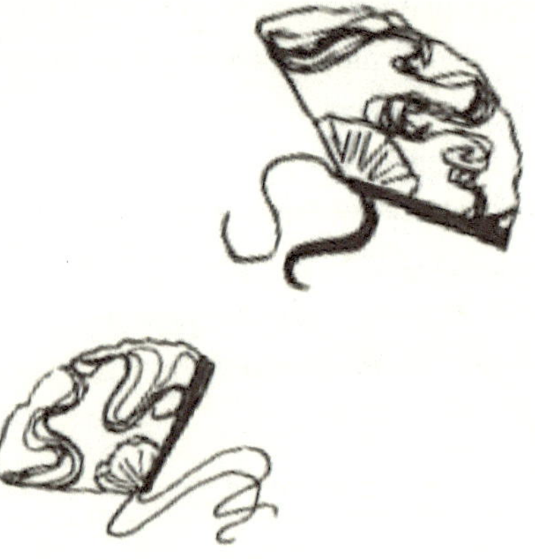

Can I take a broom in hand,
To sweep away memories that still stand,
Aches that linger within my remains
Waiting to swoop in my brain again

The hotness of tea, through my brain it flows,
Within my veins, its warmth steadily goes.
Unrequited love, a tale I've survived,
Recovering from loss, it's grip is tight
Yet, hidden within, a lingering weight,
Unrequited hate, a mystery awaits.

Life, a speed breaker, it seems,
Riding high, chasing dreams,
The climax of youth, moments so fast,
Yet be aware! it won't last.
Unaware of how time flew,
Elderness arrives, a subtle cue,
Lying on the sofa, a familiar sight,
Reflecting on life's fleeting flight.

Tried to crease the uniform fresh and crisp,
Yet the cloth remains smooth, not mine, I reminisce.
A uniform, given to be worn,
Not new, old threads, another's history borne.
Erasing books, written by hand before,
Pencil marks remain, a tale of knowledge's lore.
No new books used ones I possess,
Pens and pencils passed down, their worth I assess.

If I crave new things now, hear my plea,
Dear mother, I long for what's new and spree
Now they are within sight, I can behold,
New, neat, and clean, treasures to unfold.
Here they are now in my reach
Forever with me like a cherished dream

I sowed love in you, but reaped hatred's plight,
My heart yearned for you, every day and night,
Yet you sought distance, love's cold divide,
No wonder we crave opposites, our hearts in fight
What I sowed, I did so true,
But reaped a love I never knew.
In love's paradox, life's echoes stirred,
Deceived by the words once heard.

Almost near to making same mistake,
To open wounds that still ache.
Wounds I stitched with care
Now to be opened, my hands laid bare
Time by time, I accepted fate's decree,
But then you came, showered mercy on me.
With grace unstitched the wound,
Though it is hurting, blood spurts soon
The loose skin you peeled; a relic it seemed,
You stitched it with warmth, it's within beamed.
A rebirth; that's how you saved me,
Enabling me to meet the old me, so free.

Once there was a green tree,
Giving all its leaves to those in need,
Left with shrill stems in the end,
Once standing tall now bend
Unaware of the toll it took on the tree,
Sacrificing its own healing, for their plea.
It gave all its leaves to them,
Yet received nothing in return.
Once the giver, now at your door,
Begging for a few leaves, nothing more.

Your clamorous voice
Piercing through my brain
Never thought you will be the one
I will never see again

Once the hatchling wills
Not to leave the nest,
How come it comes to this
That he left the world,
Only to depart the nest?

When Life Gives you Lemons...
By Fakeha Imran

"When life gives you lemons...

some are sweet, some are sour."

Millions of Stars

We're millions of souls in the darkness
We're millions of people with heartache
We're millions of stars lost in the galaxy
Shining in secret
Loving in secret
Ready to be heard
Ready to be appreciated
Ready to be loved
Broken, we get lost in the darkness when we're hurt
Put back together, we shine brighter when we're loved

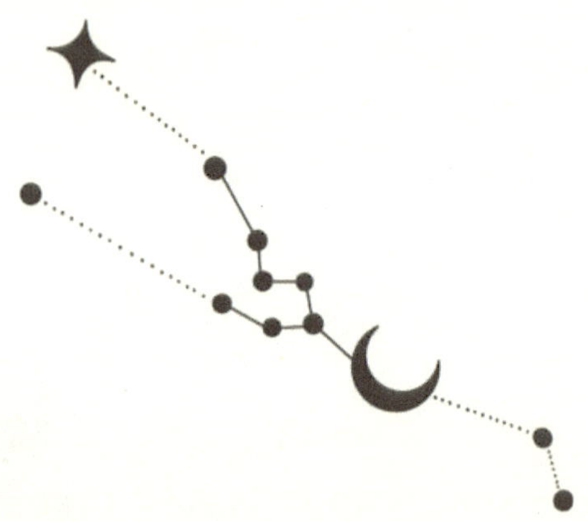

We grew up too fast

We're all moving on
With very little thought to our past
We're all moving on
And I need to know what spell was cast
We're all moving on
But I feel like we all grew up too fast

The weird calm to my storm

She's the calm to my storm
That same exact storm that we both watched unravel
The same exact storm that we both enjoyed together
"It's loud" they said
"Not as loud as those thoughts" we replied
"It's scary" they said
"Not as scary as falling this fast" we replied
"You're weird" they said as they turned to leave
"Not as weird as life" we replied
They left
We turned to look at each other
"It's funny how we're so similar yet so different..."
We both agree "we're weird"
That's what they said

Defended lies

She looked up at him with stars in her eyes
Now she looks up at him with pain, her heart broken by his lies
She trusted him with her heart
She trusted him to protect her
Little did she know it was him she needed to be protected from
He defended himself
He defended his lies
She defended him
She defended his lies
Her heart and her mind
Were at war about the wrongs and the rights
Now she looks up at him
And into his eyes
Questioning what made him lie
Questioning if he knows it is with him that her heart still lies

It’s time to move on

She told me she missed him
“What do you miss about him...?” I asked,
“The delayed replies or his pretty littles lies...?
Or maybe the flowers he never got you...?
Was it really that easy to forget you...?”
“You deserve better” I tell her, “Oh how I wish to hear the
words from you...*Maybe it’s time to move on”*
Because girl...it’s time to move on...

Stupid Cupid

She's stupid
Because she was scared
She got the cupid
Because she cared

Closure

Text him,
Text him not,
Text him,
Text him not,
All day long
She wished to confront him
She wished to have closure
Text him,
Text him not,
Text him,
Text him not,
At last, that was what she chose
To text him not
Because what was the guarantee that he'd respond
After all that he did was
Leave her texts on seen and pretend she is not
And that for her...was closure

Heart break

She gets her heart broken piece by piece
She loses the person she thought would never leave
She's having difficulty trying to believe
That the person who she trusted the most was the one who deceived
A part of her knows she should be relieved
Because with them...lies, red flags, blames was all she received
She wonders what is it that made her so naïve
She spent all her energy to grieve
Instead of on her dreams that she has yet to achieve
She has tears in her eyes
But she's laughing at the jokes
She has a smile on her face
But only a few know her heart got broke
The people she cares about the most
Are the ones who make her feel lost
The people she loves without a cost
Are the ones who hurt her the most

Shattered glass

She wonders why does she even care
When it's like walking on shattered glass with her feet bare

The art of fake smiles

She has mastered the art of fake smiles
And of the fear and sadness behind her eyes,
There is nothing but a mere reflection

False pretenses

We're two people made out of the same cloth
But we both know it's ripped into shreds
We're two people who claim to have forgotten about it
But we both know it's still in our heads
We're two people trying to keep up with each other
But we both know we're falling apart
We're two people who took back everything
But we both know we forgot to get back our hearts
We're two people who claim to be separate
But we both know we used to be one

Friends no more

BFFs
Best Friends Forever
Forever turned into never again
Friends turned into strangers again
But this time we're strangers with memories
Memories that clearly only one of us cherishes
Cherishes enough to pick up the phone and try to mend things
Mend things by calling it a misunderstanding

Maybe...Maybe...

I wish you know how much I think of you
Then maybe...maybe...you would understand
I wish I knew why I think of you
Then maybe...maybe...I would be able to let go
There are days I feel like I am going insane
Then there are days I feel numb to everything but this pain

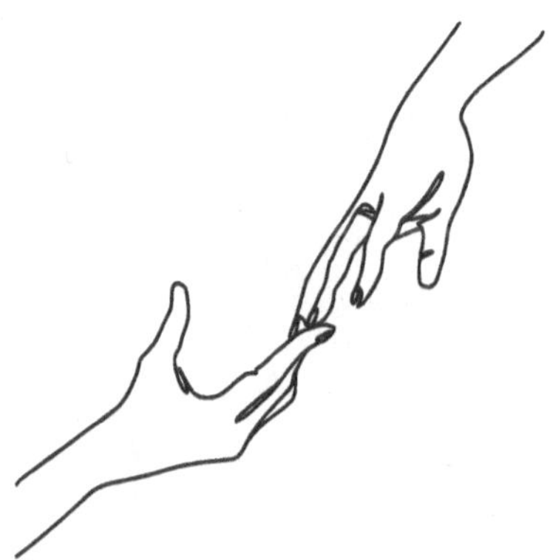

I don't love you...any less

I hope I sounded convincing when I said I don't love you
Because the truth is I cannot leave you
No matter how hard it is to speak to you everyday
No matter how bad your words hurt me in every single way
You know I cannot say goodbyes
Because I am not good at telling lies
I hope you cannot see it in my eyes
How my love for you never dies
And honestly, I must be crazy to think you'll ever put in as much effort as I did
That you'll care as much as I do
But despite all of that...the thought of you caring about me stays
Just like I know I'll love you for always
But I hope it's not for forever
And that one of these days
I find the strength I need to part ways

Raindrops

Have you ever watched the rain fall...?
Have you ever imagined each droplet to be a memory with that one person who made you love the sound of thunder...the sound of rain...that scent that indicates the clouds are crying...?
Have you ever wondered what are the clouds crying for...?
Are they crying for the memories encased in each of those droplets...?
Is letting the raindrops fall their way of reminding you of memories with that person...? To ensure none of the memories fade away...? To ensure that person does not fade away...?
Does the rain remind you of that person...?

Lost but not found

Do I want you back...?
Stupid stupid question...
Of course, I do...
Do I want you back just to lose you all over again...?
No, I don't
I can't go thru it all again
I can't lose you again
Cuz the last time I did
I lost myself as well
And I haven't found me yet...
I don't know if I ever will

I wish...

I wish I never met you
But if I look at the years I spent with you
I cannot imagine them without you
I wish I could unlove you
I wish I could erase all the memories I still cherish
I wish I could go back in time and unmeet you
But meeting you was one of the best things in my life
I wish I could go back and at least talk to you less
But talking to you was one of the best things of my everyday
I wish I could go back in time and undo what ruined us
Because that...was one of the worst things in my life

Peek or a Glance

It wasn't just romance
It was a peek or a glance
Into what we could've been
It wasn't just a dance
It was a peek or a glance
Into what our rhythm could've been
It wasn't just a glance
It was a full-blown eye contact
That left me in a trance

Priorities

You want it
But you don't
You can
But you won't
At the end, it's all about priorities

We fell together

I've been there
I've done that
I've fallen down
And I've gotten up
We fell together
But we fell apart

They got their happily ever after

He was her world
And she was his
She was the village girl
Who found her love in the big city
She found peace in him
The kind of peace that led them to their happily ever after
The happily ever after that they deserved
The kind of happily ever after where they traveled the world
Or at least a couple of countries
They got their happily ever after
With three little girls whom they adored
They got their happily ever after
The kind of happily ever after where they returned back to
the city they met in
That was also the city she lost him in
Lost him but not the memories that she will cherish forever
and ever

Veiled Reveries
By Hania

How are you so quiet about it?

How are you so quiet about it?
Your sadness I mean
How do you hold it in your bones
And not let it speak

Parts of you are left behind
In the house that you grew up in
Echoes of your laughter still haunt
The timber wood of the backyard swing

Somewhere, there's moonlight on the ocean
And the sound of heavy rain as you lay in bed
Hidden in another universe
There's a solace you haven't felt yet

July Afternoon

Its 2:47 on a July afternoon - I watch
As a child clings to her mother's finger
And something about children always
Wanting to hold
Someone's hand is really
Making me a little deranged
I don't know what it is
Or what it means
All I can say is there is a poem in here
I have not found it yet, but it is there
In the way children grip our hands so tightly
How they are so fragile and delicate
But when they hold on to things that are familiar
It's impossible to get them to let go
And nothing ever comes away unscathed
Adults are like that too
When we feel safe in something, we hold on tight
With our razor sharp talons, our daggers and knives
And something rarely comes out without claw marks on it
Someone barely makes it out alive
I don't know why but its 2:47 on a July afternoon and
Something about infants holding on unflinchingly
Makes a horrible mirror for us broken lovers' realities

Maybe I Should Have Wanted Less

Maybe I should have wanted less
Mother I know I am hungry
I take what little love I get — in my two hands
And hold on to it so tight it cannot breathe
Mother I am hungry I know
But I have never known hunger
Like the creatures that feast on my tender bones
It's a hundred teeth and yet I know
One of those belong to you
Mother you've been hungry too
This hunger is our vice
After all, I came from you
When you don't get love on a silver platter
You learn to lick it off of knives
And the thousand creatures that feast on you
And me — they know it too
That taste of retribution
And a hunger for blood on gilded spoons
There are a thousand teeth — I feel them now
And I'd let them feast on me
Let our bodies rot to corpses
In a year or a week

This Will Not Come Again

There's something about being a teenager
Sacred to those few prominent years
The precipice of adulthood, the edge of adolescence
A teenage daydream, the ache of eighteen

There's a sort of spark that no one else can see
Something that children could never grasp
And adults no longer remember
There was fury and anger, love and passion

But there was something else too
I don't think I will ever find it again
No matter how hard I look
That's a kind of time travel even photographs can't bring

Whatever it was now seems veiled
Untouchable, distant, and far removed
There was an ache of eighteen and
Looking back on it leaves me a little hollow

Because I now know — I can't go
Back to who I was before and
What the ache had meant
Was that this will never come again

I Want You To Remember Me

I want you to remember me
Keep me alive in your memory
Think of me always
Let me haunt your dreams

I want you to remember me
Keep me alive in your dreams
Let me come alive from you
Water down a steep ravine

Because those who live on
In mind and memories
Live for an eternity — through
Cotton dresses and sweater sleeves

I want you to remember me
An echo or a silent scream
Let out when you felt the ghost of me
Playing those rusting piano keys

Seven Years Old Again

Every lover you've taken
Had his weapons at the ready
With his words and righteous fury
All painting your skin so pretty

"I have so much love for you"
You're seven years old and
Your father loved you too
So you take it as a testament

Until the day finally comes
When you let your skin feel the warmth of the sun
All that's wrong is suddenly bold and true
Now that you can see it too

They find you cold and distant
But who could ask you to be bold again
When he's raising his fists and
You're seven years old again

Mary Oliver

These are the affirmations of a sinner
Tongue in cheek, blood in mouth
Through gritted teeth you whisper
"You do not have to be good"

"It is a serious thing
Just to be alive
On this fresh morning
In this broken world"

Mother

Mother she is called
Mother she is not
I don't think of you as a mother at all
Mother madness, mother blood
Mother havoc, mother corrupt
Our relation is hatred
Broken fingernails full of dried blood
Burning halos, faith unholy corrupt

Memento mori

(Translation: remember you must die)

"Remember you must die"
Like dandelions swept in the wind
Soft, light morning dew on grassy fields
And the Sun on your skin

"Remember you must die"
Like those collapsing stars of supernovas
Creating, becoming, tearing through the cosmos
And entropy and heat, chaos and physics

"Remember you must die"
Like all those here before you
Bleeding, screaming, loving, feeling till they fell
So remember to live

Even The Worst Of Me

I know it is unfair to ask you love all of me
Only a miracle can be our salvation in this misery
I couldn't have you truly
Never unconditionally, couldn't love
All of you the way you're meant to be

Still I'll crave your acceptance
And beg for scarps of your affections
To love and be loved as reverence
To hold and be held as penance
Talons digging into your flesh and tendons

This ugly desperation, ruthless salvation
And all my worthless conviction
Has been lost to some twisted declarations
Of desire and truth, oh how I wish
I could let you go without it hurting

But my love is deadly
And everything it touches turns to tragedy
With all that is revealed of my reality
Tell me you can love me, even the worst of me
Even the worst of me, even the worst of me

Make It Easy

I beg of you, make it easy
Say I never mattered
Loathe me, hate me, curse me
Tell me it was all spite and envy

We met, two Suns pouring into the world
We left, two husks charred and burnt
You loved me entirely
With everything you had to give

I loved you too
With whatever I had left
All this broken damaged mess of me
I ask you, make it easy

Say I never mattered
Say you were always meant to leave me

Curse Me With A Lukewarm Love

What is the point — of a lukewarm love?
If I am not drowning in it
Then it is not enough

Let it consume me, remake me
Wretched and monstrous, brave and bold
I am only its to mold

All the lovers of this world
All their sunlight and rain
Their thunderstorms and hurricanes

Consume them, devour them
And I too would be undone
If I were in the arms of such a tumultuous love

Hurt me, leave me, kill me if you must
But do not curse me
With a tepid, lukewarm love

Past Tense

I've always hated the past tense
Lived
Loved
Held
These stories always start from the end
And yes, all endings are new beginnings
But sometimes all they do is rot
And what has been lost
Can never be brought
Back - at least not whole
Not in the way you remembered
I've always hated the past tense
Left
Abandoned
Memorialized
Look how it takes from me
Everything becomes a memory
And then it is
Gone
Lost
Forgotten
Oh how I hate the past tense

People Have Done This Before

There's a squirrel on the tree behind your face
And a quiet wind blowing through the park at midday
It's loud and cramped and the melting —
Ice cream leaves our fingers sticky and sweet
People have done this before

It's September and your jacket keeps me warm
I take a deep breath and try to memorize it all
The smell of your perfume, the smell
Of you, and the way we're sipping coffee by the fire
People have done this before

Today the podcast we started listening to together ended
'Who could have thought we'd make it this far' 'I could've. I did'
The summer heat will — hide my blush I'm sure
Because people have done this before
But not us

Oceanic Feeling

Loving you is a grand experience
I bring you coffee in the morning and
You make us breakfast
We let the vulnerable show
The soft, tender, bruised mess of us
I hold a knife to your throat
And you would let me draw blood
You hold my heart in your hands and
I'd let you clench your fist around it
Choke me till I lose my breath
Love me till I lose myself
And after the chaos and fireworks
The whiskey, the rhythm and blues
After all the pain of our past is dead and gone
You feel it too
That oceanic feeling I feel with you
I knew it the moment our eyes met
And again when you made me laugh till I wept
And again when you smiled at me in the morning light
A sensation of eternity
Being one with the external world as a whole
That's what I feel with you
This oceanic feeling made mine through you

Cities of Poetry, Cities of Ruin

Starfall and amber skies
'Never have I ever' and little thin white lies
Soft breezes, and gentle laughter, your lovers' eyes
Crimson cheeks, sun-kissed skin
My house of art and poetry shall never see ruin

Falling bombs and nuclear clouds
'What have I done' and mindless doubts
Dead calm, a deafening screech, and another shroud
Crimson streets, fire-burnt corpses
A house of ruin, watch how it collapses

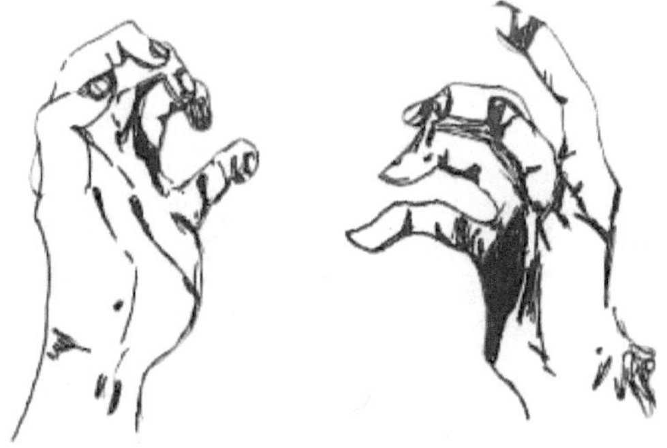

Please hold my hand/Please don't let go

Please hold my hand
Please don't let go
I know that lovers
Grow apart and grow old

And I know that time
Is cruel and it won't
Let me stay or let you go
Just because I wish it so

I may feel afraid but let us be bold
I won't let you live alone
So hold my hand and don't let go
Keep me with you wherever you go

It's because I loved you so
And you loved me too
Fate may be cruel and yet it can't
Take me away from you

To The Moon and Back, Remember?

Smile my love; I want to see the stars shine
Brighter than the night sky, one last time
Even in death I am by your side

Let's not say goodbye and just talk —
About the weather and your day at work
I'll laugh like a hapless fool and give you a smirk

You'll be brave for me and I'll be strong for you
Isn't that what we always do?
Be each other's anchors whenever we feel blue

You'll make small talk like you've got
A hundred more nights and not
Just these few hours in my arms

I know you'll be sad when I'm not around
But it'll be alright for we made a vow
To the moon and back, do you remember now?

Serene Melancholy

Oh look how she delights
Standing there in serene melancholy
Under the open sky, bathed in moonlight
Looking like every woman's envy

She'll walk by graceful as ever
Leave them stuck in fantasies and daydreams
Wishing for just one summer
Of her embrace and that cool summer breeze

Ah that serene melancholy
Something unprecedented this way comes
Divine beauty or something unholy
Swaying to the beat of the drums

A serene melancholy tune she hums
Breathless and a little drunk
On that voice and coke and rum
And you'd watch her, mystified, till kingdom come

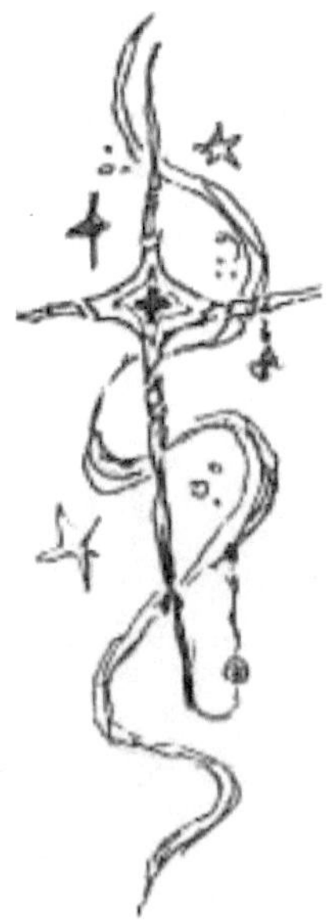

Loves Wake

Do you feel ashamed when you're
Blissfully singing the blues
And you think of my name
And the twin flame bruise

Has time taken from you
The vibrant memories of our youth
Where we stood heart in hand
Blissfully singing the blues

This is not the end, you feel it still
It comes alive, that dulling ache
Till you're blissfully singing the blues
At our loves wake

The Cryptids' Show

On stormy nights, she stirs awake
From an ancient slumber, and a vow to break
With eyes that gleam like a crimson fire
And the haunting choir of its dreadful call

In haunted mansions, her echoes moan
Resonating through halls unknown
And the cobwebs clinging to ornate walls
Shudder as she whispers in those empty halls

Beware the woods, where shadows grow
For lurking there is the cryptids show
In the moon's pale gleam, there she'll roam
Forever bound to the unknown

The Suffocating Muse

By Misbah Gul

Let me bleed with others

Let me bleed with others
Like they mourn when they lose beloved one
When they lament on sufferings
Break themselves when are deceived
Shed tears when are alone
Let me bleed with others
For me, we share the same body and pure soul
We both can feel pain in piercing heart
We live in the same home
Our origin is alike and
Philosophy of life
Let me bleed when they bleed.

Opinion changes

When they flow words for you
Tell them
They are meaning takers
and they reflect
their opinion
For opinion,
most changeable thing is
it varies with age and
Changes owing to
Wisdom added in.
So, you don't
flip your perspective
For what they believe
Don't be influenced
By what they reveal.
Time passes by and
When they are more
acknowledged of
They don't realize
What they had uttered in the past.

Dead life

Sometimes responsibilities
don't let you die
But compel you to survive,
Not to live life.
They swallow
the inner charm and
outer growth.
They make you dull and dim
Invisible pain surrounds and
Imprisons you in dark cell
where you breath
But suffocate and sigh.
They make man
A dead corpse.
If
They are fulfilled
With dissatisfaction and distress.

Sudden Upcomings

Uncertainties are real.
For those who ask
Whether misfortunes or omens occur?
Tell them
They do arrive
with their presence
Peeping from far away and
waiting for their time.
It's human who calls them
sudden upcoming.
For them
They are fixed, ordered
to happen.
Pleasant or unpleasant depends
But
They mold your every plan
Changes your directions
which weren't before
Incite and excite your emotions.
And believe in
They are worthy
They possess better plans than yours.

In Search of Peace

They search for peace
the more near and dear one
an invisible to touch and absorb
which is not settled on top of mountain
nor in opulence of world

But one who craves
fill up unseen temptations of soul
and needs of life
Who understands the nature of
free from lies and vices
peace sleeps in his arms
without knocking.

Faith in lows

In a dark prison
Blind and bare house of devils
Life blooms till hope glows.

Arcana of dark

It's better to find colors in dark
They behold
unseen patterns of essence
Some light and few heavy in
it's nature and texture
For black it absorbs
all flaws and fancy modes
mixed altogether in a dark liquor
shining in a glass
Like all glitters are combined into

For dark
there is mystery and agony
secrets embedded in walls
an enigmatic life to search in
conspiracies in a box
Packed and fixed
Striving to be revealed
And destroying whole concealed cave
made of untold tragedies.

Regain of self

What occurred was past
I know, the gray sky was on top
all the arrows were pointed
towards me
the hope was burning into ashes
the tiny spirits scattered away in air
lamppost ceased to shower rays on me
I know, the fragile and feeble
my soul was
crawling to find fair place of serenity

But, everything heals and germinates again
For time it is a great healer
So I nourished
when water was fetched
Like the dry and dead tree
regain life after autumn
I mended all torn pieces
for beauty scars are a must
Like mirror shows many reflections
when broken into parts
I gathered all strength to reappear
Like all are jumbled to become one
I stored power for my soul
So my soul reignites whole
washed out the grim and gloomy phase
Occurred in old pages.

Choices vary

Gloomy atmosphere
Fusion of rotten and rare
One gulp else blows out.

Do what you like

Do what you like
For you,
None beholds strength
None faces troubles
None bears burden
None sees wounds
None fights battle
None swallows sufferings
None listens to melodies
None admires beauty
None picks better
None catches guise
None hears whispers
None sings songs
None soars high
None touches peaks
None dives deep
None finds hidden
None walks on fire
For you,
You are the bearer of yours
Do what you like.

Behind the walls

One looks at what shown
the coloured geometry of fancy world
black layered with white
truth curtained of deceive
Pretty lies heard more
inciting face of apathy
spreading in humming air, spiced more
making it believed,
followed like ants in clan
taken away the sweet reality in smooth way
One looks at what is served on a plate.

But what's invisible in
thickness of fake echoes
trembling sounds of worth crashed
when collide
Unable to reach for
what they meant
bright eyes, blind though
can't seek what hoped
rushed truth stuck in twisted crowd
Unable to travel for
what it survived
Scorching lights barely showing the path
One dies enough by
knowing the dark
Apparent better hides the inner chaos.

Fear of soaring

Calm and plain blue sky
an urge to flap wings and soar
But scared to fall down.

Dying Voice

Shivering body, crippled soul
Fluttering heart, terrible thoughts
Besieged by thorns, laid on stones
painful waves whizzing into ears
one in a deep slumber
test of conscience
To face or blow apart
Like a black sheep, does when prey
Or become a goddess, liberates from cage
Listen unheard what to say
Or sleep
just another injured on the way.

Silence

Listen to what can't be heard
an enormous language enveloped there
torn body, chained soul, and caged spirits revolving here
Listen to what can't be heard
enough tension compressed there
lot of voices buried and juggling thoughts running here
Listen to what can't be heard
embedded pain and destruction built there
Long cries, deep breaths, and heavy tears shredded here
Listen to what can't be heard
Frosted air, sheer emotions roaming there
patience dies, twinkling pieces of hope burn, and faith vanishes here
For the melodies, unheard are sweeter
Listen to what can't be heard.

Hidden Stories

face with expressions
Venting shallow and deep curves
Countless tales masked up.

Bonds

loyal blood relations of love and care,
strengthened by happiness shared, sorrows consoled,
trusted to reveal what one suffers from,
stand by when the storms get high.

small Quarles and loud voices;
harsh speaks, bitter lies, when ignited within clan,
destroy essence and violate bonds,
a lot of suffering and many drown.

Arcana of the Heart

by Qania Murtaza

From clay to love icon

Come on little heart
Let's take a start
Bring some dune
From pretty lune
Let's make two idols
'You' and 'I' will be the title
Come on little heart
Let's take another start
Do something like this
Bring these idols and dismiss
Knead the soil again
Create two idols in lane
Now, one like me,
One like you
Find something in me,
And I can in you

Labyrinth of life

In the sublime vista
Where sky meets terra

Time seems to stand still
When golden rays behold Sierra

In the whirl of plumage thrive
The hues of a mortal's drive

In the echoes of serenity boom
The yearn for resilience and resume

In the flickering wicks of candle
Uncertainty of life makes a scandal

All these merged to make an adventure
To paint a picture of misery and rapture

In the heart of shadow

When I see myself in the dark
I ponder how mites survive in the bark

Unsheltered thoughts seem to shatter
With the rattling sound of clatter

The keen intuition of mystics reveals
How a bleeding soul, the night heals

In the cover of night, two souls embrace
Bound by love, intertwined in space

"Life attracts life" same is the case
Sunflowers smile on bright days

You and I

You and I,
Like a couple of roses on tips
Blooming with enchanting beauty I cherish,
The beauty that takes away all sorrows
The beauty that heals the wounded souls

You and I,
Like the colors of a painting on canvas
Pacifying one's piercing eyes I admire,
In the vibrant hues, I am immersed
As one plunges into wonders of river

You and I,
Like the cottage of shared love, where
Its coziness mimics the warmth of love
Amidst whispers and laughter, we find solace,
In each word exchanged, our hearts intertwined with grace

Resonance of Agony

With desolate pain in her brain
And nostalgic sights in her eyes
She carries crushed memories
Shrieks, shrieks, and shrieks

As she passes through the gate of past
Something anchors her feet very fast
The devastating recollection of mischief
Shrieks, shrieks, and shrieks

As trapped as a fly in the web of a spider
She dares to break the norms, a resilient fighter
Choking her throat she speaks
Shrieks, shrieks, and shrieks

Whispers of Yesterday

When the mornings were cheerful
When the nights were dreamful
Fair and starry, it was when
I was a child, I was blissful

When life was meaningful
When the death was mournful
Lively and dreadful, it was when
I was a child, I was blissful

When the spirits were high
And the souls were truthful
Dainty and beautiful, it was when
I was a child, I was blissful

Luminous Canvas of Youth

What example should I give of your youth?
A human has become, like Kiran Mahtab, forsooth

In the face has melted the beauty of the graceful moonlight's glow
In the eyes resides the ecstasy of the youthful night garden's show

A bent stem, the neck portrays, like a rose's gentle grace,
Sun's candle flickers a hundred times, casting its radiant embrace

When the tresses unfurl, evening's heart emits a sigh
Touch the ground, bow down, and watch the sky rise high

You are the image of the dream of my paradise,
What comparison can I give for your youthful guise?

Raising and Erasing Biases

There is a new drop in the river
Here is a strange shadow in the desert

There flows the water of wisdom
To sate the ravenous for lore

In the whispers of their minds, the secrets hide
Ancient truths of knowledge, they do confide

Here prevails darkness and disease
A land of forlorn, a land of blocked breaths

That breathless land where the forlorn reside
A place of restructuring, where ambitious suicide

Let bridges be built, let symphony portray
Let catharsis be brought, let's embrace gray

Lingering Gloom of Past

In a far-away land,
Great mysteries of nations expand
In the pyramids of Giza stand
The enigmatic graveyard of grand

Embedded with concealed charm
They coerce the Tanoura to perform
The deed of thrill and no harm
To retain the spirit serene and calm

The custodian of chronicles communicate
Tales of times, they resonate
Yet shadows cast, a somber weight,
History's burden, a haunting fate.

Burial

And when I die, imprison me
Like a dried flower in a book of love
When you ever get leisure in life
Remember me in the decayed leaves of this book,
Releasing its fragrance in your breath,

Or bury me else in such a place,
Where there are mountains all around
Where the springs make beautiful a sound
Where the caravans of jackals howl at night
And butterflies fly by day and dance

Or bury me where,
the ugly feelings of death do not dwell
If you cannot do that, then
Bury me somewhere in the thick forest
Where the travelers reach under the tree and lose the way
And unknowingly raise their hands to pray

If you cannot do that,
Bury me in the story where
Characters die but love lives forever
If you cannot do even this,
Just bury me in your heart because
Your heart will be the only place to die.

Unwoven Tapestries

By Sarah Malik

Let your hair down Rapunzel

In the present era, there exists
A modern day Rapunzel's tale persists
Not trapped in a tall tower built of stone
But in her own mind, she's stands alone
Her aspirations spread like hair so fair
In cascading dreams, she remains unaware
A stream of thoughts flows free and wide
Yet her fears force her to hide
The tower of doubt holds her tight
The unknown fills her heart with fright
Will history repeat itself? No
Go recognize your true self
O Rapunzel, untie your braid of might
Release your potential that's kept out of sight
Break the chains that confine your soul
And let destiny's winds take control
Let your hair down Rapunzel for once
Let everyone see you are not a dunce
Embrace the journey without fear
Your destination is very near
Discover the world that awaits you
A tale untold, bold and true

Closure

A single blood drop
Remains in the heart I owned
Lost, a life once known

A train to nowhere

Sweeping past the lush green meadows
Whistling a symphony of ambitions
Echoing with gentle titters and sweet giggles
A train carried souls hopeful and bright
Filled with dreams or rather delusions
Unmatchable aspirations and unbroken vigor

But things were expected to take an unexpected turn
The sight of budding wildflowers
And unfiltered rays of sunlight
Was soon to vanish forever
Innocence would dissipate before long
The purity in the air was to evaporate

Leaving behind the monstrous smoke
Ready to engulf every ounce of simplicity
The heads were to be devoid of hearts
The once genuine smile were to be
Intertwined with melancholic sighs
Alas the train journeyed to nowhere's end,
A search for fulfilment yet around the bend.

Change

Dancing golden leaves,
Shift nature's course, twirling on winter's
Gently whispered breath.

Deception

Masks appear on stage
Enacting the old wives' tales
Masquerading as truth

Illusion

A trail of broken promises
A tale of missed opportunities
With shattered trust
Trace a series of illusion
Looms over a cloud
Ready to burst
All the mirth
Over saddened faces
And empty eyes
They embrace themselves
Thinking of it as a delusion

Up above in the lonely sky
Roams a stranded cloud
Tracing a series of illusions
A tale of missed opportunities
A trail of broken promises
It makes a plea
To blank faces with
Shattered trust
To allow it to burst
One last time
To shower all its assets
Over the barren crust

Nature's Brilliance

With soft petals and vibrant hues
Stands a flower away from other queues
It glitters in the yellow sunset
It heals scars one can bet
For nothing can resist its charm
To stressed nerves it acts as a balm
It shakes gently with the breeze
Pretending to be a harmless tease
To gales it stands as a figure of resilience
It is an embodiment of nature's brilliance

Brittle Beings

Frail souls we are
Lurking in the wilderness
In search of solace

Brown

A hue of warmth
An earthly tone
A subtle expression
A secret keeper

Runs in the veins of leafs
Stands in the trunk of trees
Resides in South Asian skin
Face of seed and ties
Narrator of roots and soils

Horse's drape
Autumn's attire
Walnut's core
Almond's peel
A chocolate delight
A palette's pride

Soberly wears nature's crown
Such is the colour brown

Modern Man

Composed of digits
Dreams of wires and lights
Entangled, confused

Nature's Canopy:

A canopy of boundless blue
That encompasses us day and night
It is where dreams and birds take flight
Haven for poets and poetic souls
The sky stands tall above us

It is where moon casts its silver glow
And sun shines bright
Exhibiting nature's might
Here stars twinkle and planets reside
And meteors take glide

Nature's limitless canvas it is
A depiction of rhyme and reason
Freedom for all it chants
It echoes with beautiful melodies
And presents an enchanting celestial dance

Reminiscing

In this bustling city where life now thrives
Every passing second we struggle to strive
From dawn to dusk we run and race
Unable to sit and enjoy nature's embrace
Amidst the chaos moments fade like mist
But in some point of life we fail to persist
We then trace our lives back to the time
When everything that existed was sublime
Like sand in an hourglass sifts away
One grain after another passes a day
O bring back that those unrushed evenings
Those peaceful mornings those calm springs
Let's bring back that forgotten solitude today
Let's break free from pace and sit down to stay

Enigma

Standing straight
Almost motionless
Lost in thought
With a blank face
And questioning eyes
The mirror inquired
Who are you?
Silence prevailed
The air was stagnant
Once again the mirror
Received no answer

Abstract Art

On a canvas set ablaze
By lines that make a maze
With colors so dark and bold
Narrating stories all untold
Shapes presenting a strange dance
Within a moment you're in the trance
Representing ideas so unique
Creating an image so picturesque
Each stroke so fierce yet delicate
Making the design detailed and intricate
Voicing every emotion so loud and clear
Exhibiting a spectacle so rare
Behind every piece there is a scheme
That transports you into a daring dream
It makes its way from eyes to heart
This is the power of abstract art

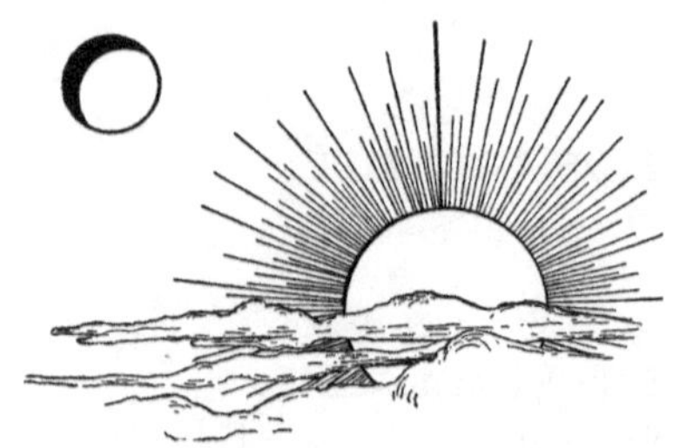

Untitled

Present once there was a figure
Lurking as a shadow of mystery
Before the same dame it once besieged
Stood there the shadow again
Darkened by the luminous sun
Whispers conquered the town
But not the dame
For times had changed
Spring was long forgotten
The rumors of its rebirth
Had long been silenced
Hope was laughed upon
The wait was futile
The shadow blew the candle
And all the fire that once burnt
Hearths and hearts both
Was set out at last

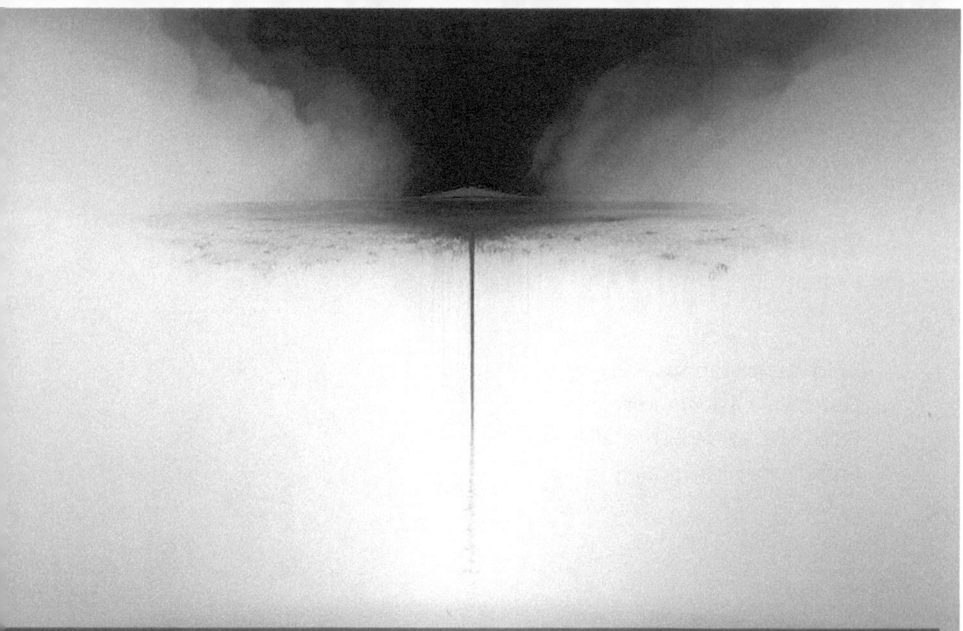

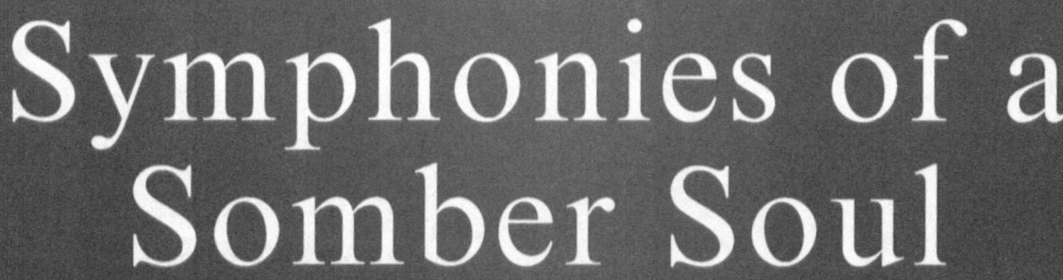
Symphonies of a
Somber Soul
By Ukasha Wadood

The Floral Face

Precious, peerless petals sway
Festooned on her flowery face
Blood-red, my woes they allay
Entrancing with uncanny grace

An Ode to Enamoring Eyes

Under the shade of black brows
Glowing orbs flicker, untold
Washing away all one's woes
And tell what your future holds

Hear, hear as I proclaim
Those entrancing eyes shame
Moons, stars, and all the same
Melting hearts with a fierce flame

Hear, hear as to you I convey
Tales of two shells that stun and sway
Soothing souls with surreal joy
Slain souls whose loss none could allay

Of these fair, amorous eyes do I sing
So long as my soul and my body cling

An Autumn Eve

Behold the gentle belle with a stunning stride
Donning cherry crimson, delicate dame dances
Catches my earthly eye but only a short sight
Her dark locks, lingering like lethal lances

A gentle autumn breeze teases her silky locks
Her fingers rest on her temples,
Those scarlet cheeks with all their gloss
Stupefy the onlookers of deep dimples

As she strolls, the fortunate leaves fall
For her gaze sets ablaze every heart
Her features tender, her stature tall
Yet she tears a thousand hearts apart

Away with the setting sun, she goes
Her frame redder than fading fireball
Forsaking me with nothing but woes
Granting not even her name to call

Dwells does she in my daring dreams
In my heart, her gleeful gaze gleams

Life

The drops leave the clouds
In tandem, they meet their demise
- The cycle takes its course

Weeping Clouds

Pray, tell what it is that ails thee
Sobbing slowly for all to see?
Is it wicked wind, tearing trees
Or the lightning, lambasting leaves?

Here, I, thy wail with earnest ear
Which cannot even my horrid heart bear
But it spots a familiar sight
A somber soul far from home's delight

Hope

I see leaves turning pale
I see the shine of stars fade
Falling leaves like a blade
Cut open the earth's veil

Like a vicious venom in the body
Gloom stuns the senses, spreading everywhere
And scouring ceaselessly finds a knotty
Nexus of distress, layer 'n layer

Like a king, my people sing
My praises endear me
And like a king, I, in the midst
Of heaps, am alone and free

Like a sad sailor, I sit
On my abode staring sea
Silence, serenity, worth, wit
Of what purpose are they to me?

I have no enemies but me
No flower of hope nor a tree
Does now in my heart find glee
Nor does it attempt to flee

No knock on the door does now my ear keep
In the noise of the streets, I wearily weep

Echoes of Ethereal Eyes

Rude, unruly sun
Why do you yet tirelessly try
Me, on a day so dull and dry
When untold agonies surround
All awake and all who yet lie

Cruel, callous sun
Expect me not to forsake my bed
And the dreams of the woman in red
As the world of matter is thus wound
To breed a stale state of death and dread

Haughty, horrid sun
Show me not the sweet, singing birds
Or the dancing leaves or open buds
My lone heart, blind to sight, deaf to sound
In silent ruin, against thorns, thuds

Weary, watchful sun
If her Elysian eyes you survive
Pray, tell to what blessed place does she strive
If the place be mine own to be found
Do speak or never find any shrive

Tender Hands and Winter Nights

Cold and lifeless is a winter night
Colder still is my body and soul; devoid
Of the warmth and delight
Your touch, so polite, provides

Those tender, delicate hands excite
When do they so enchantingly invite
Mine; verses longer than the winter night
Do they with such life, recite

My love, set my heart alight
With your burning life as I tried
But without you cannot survive
The cold and lifeless
That is the winter night

O the reason my heart beats and breathes. O the reason it skips a beat. O who taught me what it means to love. What it means to smile and submit to love. How love is a spell that slays its foes but stuns those who embrace it. How it is a shield that protects against the perils and strife of life. How it is a mirthful melody that silences the discordant voices of doubt, distrust, and death. How it expands and encompasses the entirety of existence.

It is you, my object, my Muse, my inspiration, my voice, my heart and soul, my whole being, my source of solace, my purpose and goal, the one who makes me feel alive. You, my darling!

The Melody of Tranquil Meadows

Let me tell you about a trip I took
Down by the meadows and the brimming brook
Gleaming greenery wherever I look
A place part of some fantastical book

Here tall figures of green
Stand straight but, in between
Some with their burden, lean
And ask you where've you been

Pillows of amicable air
Grand groups of green carpets appear
Where wary, inquiring eyes stare
A bevy of beings, far and near

My inner eye filled with blithe,
Waves wilfully with the breeze
Hymning birds and rustling leaves
Put a troubled heart at ease

But I must move on to my misery
My life has, to death, promised to keep

Come and put the moon to shame
Come and hear songs of praise
Come into my heart and dictate
My actions on the life's stage

O stars, guide me to the place where she dwells
Gaze not in her dark eyes, eyes like devouring wells
For each holder of those precious pearls tells
Tales of a peerless pulchritude that forever swells

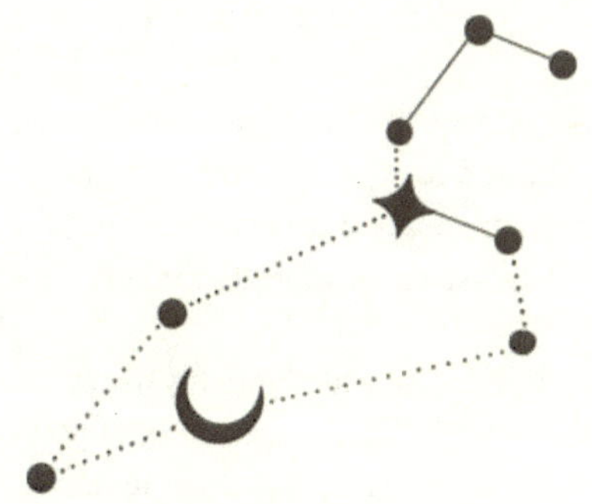

A SOOTHING EMBRACE

Turning my earthly eye to the spiritual, erring,
Anguish, agony, failure, a fault I find
Numbing my existence like a ritual, recurring
Overcome with ordeals, my faith turns blind

A state of senseless struggle in the air,
As I am pushed purposefully into the pit
On the verge, a figure lays itself bare
Mocking me as a manifestation of my wit

In the midst of madness, a mellow hand,
Heralding a respite from the grim grief,
With its tender texture erased my pang,
Vouchsafing my being a brief relief

Thence, she descended into my heavy heart,
As rain with its sublime richness showers life,
Like a Muse, she inspires my inner bard,
And in her remembrance, I forget my strife

Cruel Nights and Coveted Eyes

Foggy are these nights, obscured;
Foggier still is your notion, poured
In my mind, shadow of its pure
Surreal self; the chilling winds allure,
The mist drops seduce towards your
Warm hands; hands that no longer reassure
This heart haunted by horrid woes
And covets thy eyes, sparkling like stars
And the eyes which have equal but sparse

Rebirth

Sunken in the abyss of dark despair,
Stubbornly had the sunset on my mirth
Pain and dismay pursued me everywhere
As suffocation and smart formed the earth

My inner orchard lost its curator,
Air lost its sweeteners as birds had fled
Leaves paled as testified by the orator
Trees wore parched lips and my heavy heart bled.

As I neared my demise, these lifeless eyes
Espied a silver lining; in the morn
Clouds burst, drops tipped, birds rearrived, all lies
And woes washed away by the love: reborn

World of Woes

Trapped in the dark, dungeons of tattered thought
Detained by my mind's decrepit shackles
Like Belial, I lie with void and naught
Smarted by a slain soul's hollow hackles

Struggling to gather my broken pieces
I find my ruptured limbs in raw revolt
The tempest fire burns bones but deices
Not the frozen heart nor its lifeless vault

No hope breeds on these barren, sterile lands
No expectations plague them, no demands

Printed and Bound by ***Passive Printers*** - www.passiveprinters.com
Printing press that offers Print on Demand (POD) Facility.
Printed in The Islamic Republic of Pakistan.

www.ingramcontent.com/pod-product-compliance
Lightning Source LLC
LaVergne TN
LVHW091324150826
845673LV00006B/1758

* 9 7 8 9 6 9 7 4 9 2 5 7 2 *